3

Messages

From God

3

Messages From

GOD

**Read in an Hour
Remember for a Lifetime**

Sandy Forsythe

3 Messages From God

All Scripture verses are taken from the NIV Bible

ISBN# 978-1-7324362-0-6 (For Print book)
ISBN# 978-1-7324362-1-6 (For eBook)

First Edition

All proceeds from this book will go to support the work of Share God With Us. Our ministry shares God's Word by donating Scripture cards to both individuals and organizations across the USA, Europe, Africa and Russia. We also collect stories of God's intervention in today's world and post them on line to share the hope he gives us as we encourage others in His Love. To learn more, or to order Scripture cards, go to www.ShareGodWithUs.com.

www.ShareGodWithUs.com

Endorsements

Sandy's book, *3 Messages*, is an easy to read reminder to get back to the basics of our walk of faith. She uses practical examples of seeing God's hand in our everyday life and cherishing these sweet gifts each time. Even more, she refocuses our personal experiences back to God's Word as we are called to slow down and tell others about this amazing gift. This little book will help you redirect your daily life to praise the King, accept these gifts, recognize the practical tools He gives you to fight discouragement, and to share the gospel of Jesus Christ with confidence.

P. Stan Keith,
President and Chief Executive Officer, The Hope Center.
Dallas TX

"*Loved 3 Messages from God!* I read it this morning during my devotions and it so blessed me! I especially love the 9 words, they are such great words to live by! My prayer is that God would use this book to be a blessing to all who read it as it did me!"

Pastor David Wilson,
Senior Pastor, New Hope Chapel, Norwell MA.

"Thinking of Sandy Forsythe and reading *3 Messages from God* brings a smile to my heart. Sandy's open, vulnerable, and honest style of writing bring credibility to the beautiful book God has given her. Applying the principles, she shares in the book will equip you to live a life filled with His love...and the joy of sharing His love with others."

Edwina Patterson
Conference speaker, author, radio host, and founder of Redeeming the Time ministry. Lone Oak TX. Her Bible studies are full of truth and power.

"This little book, *3 Messages from God*, by Sandy Forsythe, is a must read for anyone who wants to gain a deeper understanding of the Trinity. All my life I have been confused by this divine concept. The picture of the Trinity depicted in the book *3 Messages*, is the clearest, most beautiful and insightful description of this mystery that I have ever encountered. I highly recommend it – it is a spiritual work of art.

Loretta Anderson,
Retired Professor of Accounting, Richland College, DCCCD, Dallas Texas. Stage IV cancer survivor.

Dedication

To the unknown woman who gave me a prophetic word over a decade ago, to live as a colander, and to let God's love flow through my life.

Table of Contents

Faithful Rose's Prayer:

That God would establish this writing, that it may be effective, and that the people reading it will be touched in such a way that they want to share it with a friend.

"Fills me in a different way."

Rose Bonica

Tying it all Together

I can assure you that God listens to our prayers. He listened to mine, and then *he answered me!* I shouldn't have been astounded, but I was. All three times. The small primer you hold is the result of me being compelled to share what he told me. It was a reluctant work of this 'normal mom,' whose goals have never included—writing something—that would have been the furthest thing from my mind.

Honestly, I'm humbled beyond recognition, as I understand how wild and grandiose this whole 'Share God's Message' sounds! Yet, I've been given this task, and I pray I'll do justice to it. This book can be read under an hour, but it contains the potential to bless you and your family for a lifetime. I pray that this is true for you as well.

His answers are profoundly simple.

How this came to be:

First, he gave me a flash vision about a windmill, and he kindly explained how it was a picture of the Trinity.

Next, he answered my lifelong question as to what I should do with my life. He simply gave me nine words that hold the key to living well for him.

And finally, he gave me a child's view of the protection he offers us each day. I was having trouble remembering the Armor of God, so he gave it to me in modern day language.

I can't stress enough how humbled I am to be given this chance to share what I believe is his message for us today. Simply put: live in awe, live pleasing him, and live under his protection. That's the message he gave me to share.

In Awe of my Father King,

Sandy

1ˢᵗ Message

An Ancient Windmill
—A Vision of the Trinity

An Ancient Windmill
—A Vision of the Trinity

Once upon a time, in a wood far, far away, I went to be alone with God. Just the two of us. I sat near a small brook, it was beautiful. Praying, I just wanted to pause and listen to God. I was still for quite a while; just as I was about to leave, he gave me a vision—the first and only one I've ever had.

It came in the blink of an eye, but even though it's been years, I can still see every detail clearly like it occurred to me just a moment ago. I want to share it with you, but I worry because it was so dreamlike that expressing it accurately may be impossible. Yet, I must try.

The vast meadow was both gold and purple, tall grasses swaying in the breeze. One second lavender-purple, another second it became summer gold. Both colors at once.

On the soft curve of the land, an ancient windmill stood—

it looked enormous, yet it fit perfectly in the landscape. I could

tell it had been there for what looked to be the beginning of time.

The breeze gently turned the wooden sails pumping fresh water.

At the foot of the windmill, there were groups of young girls,

twirling in the meadow. Holding hands, skirts fluttering,

spinning around and around in utter joy.

Laughter filled the air.

'This is so beautiful!' my spirit gasped. I asked God, 'What does this mean?'

Then he shared with me this insight: **It's a vision of the Trinity!** The windmill turns the wind into power, and that power pumps the water of life. The windmill, the wind and the water – it's a picture of the Trinity.

God, Our Abba Father: As Steady and Constant as a Windmill

The Ancient of Days was camouflaged as a humble, ancient windmill - always in view, yet graciously unpretentious. A windmill is immovable and so is God. He is our stable anchor in the shifting journey of life.

Just as a windmill was a constant signpost in the landscape for our forefathers, God directs our lives if we pay attention to where he is pointing us.

Our forefathers depended on a windmill for power, for water, the basic sustaining elements of life. In the same way, we depend on God for every aspect of our lives, whether we acknowledge him or not.

The Holy Spirit: The Wind of the Holy Spirit Powers Our Lives

The sails of the windmill turn and adjust to catch as much wind as possible. Like a windmill yielding to the wind, our lives need to turn and follow the direction(s) God gives us.

The power transfers to us when we obey and go the way he is directing us. Unceasingly, a windmill transforms the God-sent wind into power – a power that we can tap into and use in our everyday lives. You see, we all must go through God to be eternally transformed. It is the direction of the 'wind' that changes our direction. Oftentimes we need to trim our sails to follow the flow of the Holy Spirit.

Jesus Christ: The Wellspring of Life

The pure water being pumped out of the ground by the windmill is a picture of Jesus.

Just as he rose from the dead to eternal life, the windmill's water, pumped up from the ground, is a picture of our Lord— The Risen Christ.

"...but whoever drinks the water I give him will never thirst. Indeed, the water I give him will become in him a spring of water welling up to eternal life." John 4:14

He is the water of life. He freely gives us this water. Praise God!

He alone fills us with his life-sustaining water and gives us new life.

Understanding the Trinity

Our God is a triune God with three distinct parts of ONE Godhead. It is a mystery that is inconceivable to our human minds, but God is above our thinking. Comprehending God's greatness is hard.

If we could understand completely, would that be the God you'd want to worship as King and Lord of your life? How incomprehensible is it that our God is so vast and uncontainable that one being can't hold all of him? He is three, but still one.

"For there are three that testify: The Spirit, the water and the blood, and the three are in agreement." 1 John 5:7-8

A.W. Tozer said in his timeless book, *The Knowledge of the Holy*[i]

"God cannot so divide Himself that one Person works while the other is inactive."

In other words, the Trinity doesn't have conference calls with multiple parties on the line. They are ONE. They work together seamlessly, like the wind, the windmill and the water pump. Each distinct, yet all one, creating power-giving life.

A windmill's purpose is altruistic. It humbly serves those depending on it for life. It provides water and power to sustain our lives. It provides a landmark, giving an anchor in the ever-changing landscape of the world in which we live. And it can represent an eternal picture of the Trinity.

May you be blessed by the gentle force of the Holy Spirit wind,

May the Father transform you with his power, and

May the water of Christ give you eternal life.

2nd Message

9 Words

—What Should I do LORD?

What Should I do LORD?

9 Words to Live By

After a lifetime of wondering what I was supposed to do with my life, I finally came to God one morning in prayer and asked, *"What should I do LORD?"*

I had been taught at a woman's retreat to write the questions I have for God in the middle of a blank piece of paper. After writing it down, I was asked to pray and jot down anything that comes to mind. Well, it didn't take long to see God's reply! I must admit, I was a bit stunned when I looked at the page in my journal, as he had given me a map of how to please him in my life.

Amazingly, God gave me nine words as a guide on how to live and love well. They are not for me alone, but for everyone. I've thought a lot about each word over the past few years and I pray that my attempt to share what God has shown me, will help you to know and love him more deeply. With these key words, may you live each day to the fullest in joy and love.

When I asked: *'What should I do, LORD?'* He answered giving me simple keys to living well and pleasing him. (As written in my prayer journal on October 16, 2014.)

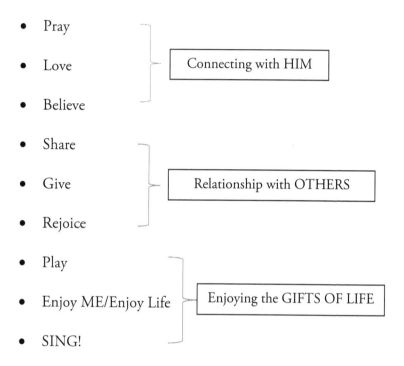

- Pray

- Love   Connecting with HIM

- Believe

- Share

- Give   Relationship with OTHERS

- Rejoice

- Play

- Enjoy ME/Enjoy Life   Enjoying the GIFTS OF LIFE

- SING!

These nine words, in this order, have helped me realize how simple he wants me to live. I believe this is how he wants all of us to live. These words are easy-to-understand directions for living well for him. With these nine words, he tells us to be channels of HIS LOVE to OTHER PEOPLE and to ENJOY LIFE

Putting These Nine Words into Action

Below are my takeaway "messages" from each of the words he has given me. I'll share these straight from my heart in the hopes that each word touches your heart too.

PRAY

When I pray, am I asking God, "What can he do for me?" or, "What can I do for him?" I need to ask myself, am I requesting or worshiping?

I know he wants my worship more than my list of requests, yet I get this wrong most days. I hurry a prayer something like: "Give me...Help me...Guide me...And oh, and please bless my family and friends." But when we pray, I believe we're supposed to be in worship, not just come to him as beggars looking for a quick fix.

My good friend, Edwina Patterson, taught me that "*It's the quality of our private time with God that determines our public value to him.*"[ii] I should think about this when I take time to really pray and not just shoot off an emergency request, expecting good results. I need to ask myself, "*Am I honoring him or demanding of him when I pray?*"

Decades ago, Edwina taught me to pray "ACTS."

First, give **ADORATION**.

Next, give deep and specific **CONFESSION**.

Third, **THANK** him for his generous gifts,

And finally, ask or give **SUPPLICATION** for my needs.

Oh, I wish that I'd pray this way each day! When I do pray like this, I can hardly get past the confession part without simply being so humbled that I never ask for more. His forgiveness is, and always has been, enough.

Scripture Verses for the Word Pray

- If my people, who are called by my name, will humble themselves and pray and seek my face and turn from their wicked ways, then I will hear from heaven, and I will forgive their sin and will heal their land. 2 Chronicles 7:14

- Do not be anxious about anything, but in everything, by prayer and petition, with thanksgiving, present your requests to God. Philippians 4:6

14

- Be joyful always, pray continually; give thanks in all circumstances, for this is God's will for you in Christ Jesus. 1 Thessalonians 5:16-18

LOVE

God's love for us is so significant. Our very heartbeat and breath depend on his grace each moment of our lives, yet we ignore him most of the time. Thankfully, Jesus doesn't prorate his love. He doesn't selfishly guard it or hold any back. He gave himself completely so that we can share eternity with him freely. He obeyed his father's will—to come out of heaven with one mission—to *pay for us.* His obedience cost him his life. Yet, he paid our sin debt because he knew we would incinerate in front of God our Father without his love covering us as a shield. The Father God, accepted his son's sacrifice given on our behalf. That is love… His love for us knows no limit. True love always has a cost attached to it; it's sacrificial.

The simple but hard truth is, if we show up at the throne of God without first confessing our need to be saved at the foot of Jesus' cross, we'll be eternally lost. We need the cover of love to enter eternity, and that cover of love is the blood he shed for us on the cross.

We need to realize that we need to be saved—only Jesus can save us from what we face in eternity. How painful our eternity will be if we disregard his sacrifice for us. If this weren't so, he wouldn't have had to come to earth in the first place. The love of Jesus changes everything.

We are called to love as Jesus loves. But honestly, sometimes, I wonder, 'Why can't I love deeply?' I have wonderful people in my life, yet I keep my heart plastered over, closed to visitors. Do you ever feel like this? I hope not, but sadly, I must admit, I sometimes do. So, once again, I asked God a question, 'Why can't I feel love?'

God answered me by helping me find the answer in his Word. I came upon several verses in 1 Peter 4, and as I read, he let me dive deep into the Scripture to see the answer: *If I want to know love, I must first love and serve others.*

I'm not a theologian, so I'm thankful God made his Word clear to me. I'll give you the Scripture passage and then I'll abbreviate my thoughts as to how I learned a profound love lesson from 1 Peter 4:2-10 – on how to live pleasing God.

Scripture and Lessons Learned

As a result, he does not live the rest of his earthy life for evil human desires, but rather for the will of God. 1 Peter 4:2

- o Lesson Learned: Live for the will of God – Don't focus on what I want, put GOD FIRST.

Above all, love each other deeply, because love covers a multitude of sins. 1 Peter 4:8

- o Lesson Learned: LOVE EACH OTHER deeply- Love others more than self.

Each one should use whatever gift he has received to serve others, faithfully administering God's grace in its various forms. 1 Peter 4:10

- o Lesson Learned: Use my gifts to SERVE OTHERS.

So, if I want to know how to love deeply, I need to put God first, set myself aside, and serve others. It sounds simple—yet I stumble all the time. But that is precisely how Jesus loved us. This is his pattern for love. This is the key to deep love.

Scripture Verses for Love

- • Love the LORD your God with all your heart and with all your soul and with all your strength. Deuteronomy 6:5

- On that day you will realize that I am in my Father, and you are in me, and I am in you. Whoever has my commands and obeys them, he is the one who loves me. John 14:20-21

- As the Father has loved me, so have I loved you. Now remain in my love. John 15:9

- If you obey my commands, you will remain in my love, just as I have obeyed my Father's commands and remain in his love. John 15:10

- My command is this: Love each other as I have loved you. John 15:12

BELIEVE

Belief is a tricky thing as you *can act like* you truly believe, but it's not proven until you're in a crisis.

I like this quote from Dr. James Denison:

"Faith is most needed when it's most challenged."[iii]

I keep this little quote on my piano, so I see it regularly. I need the reminder to make sure I'm not just going through the motions of faith, but that I truly believe what I profess. Do I honestly believe, *or do I just think I believe?*

I understand it's valuable to ask ourselves what we genuinely believe from time to time. We need to ask ourselves, *'What am I willing to die for?'* Many Christians across the globe know this because they are facing brutality daily for the honor of Christ. They know, *"It is better to die for something than to live for nothing."*[iv]

Our belief needs to be intentional and focused. It takes work and honest reflection. What we believe makes all the difference in how we live each day, and it determines who we worship or even if we worship. With a sincere belief in God, we can live peacefully even in this tumultuous world.

You see, a crisis simply reveals what we believe, and it always show a person's true character. So, I challenge you, take some time today to answer for yourself: "When I meet Jesus face to face, will he find the kind of believing faith that counts on him despite all the world's confusion?" [v]

A good friend recently shared this quote with me, "If you don't stand for something, you'll fall for anything." [vi] I hope you'll get to know what you stand for.

Scripture Verses for Believe

- "… I will come to you and fulfill my gracious promise to bring you back to this place. For I know the plans I have for you," declares the LORD, "plans to prosper you and not to harm you, plans to give you hope and a future." Jeremiah 29:11

- Jesus answered, "The work of God is this: to believe in the one he has sent." John 6:29

- May the God of hope fill you with all joy and peace as you trust in him, so that you may overflow with hope by the power of the Holy Spirit.' Romans 15:13

SHARE

I find it hard to distinguish between sharing and giving. But God gave me both words distinctly, so I've had to pray and listen intently to decern the difference. I've realized that *sharing* is an act of the heart; it's a deep wanting to have someone else enjoy what I have. When I share, it makes my heart happy. Somehow, when I share, I get back more than I've given.

We can share our concerns, our love, our heartaches, our joys. We can share our time, our money, skills, and talents. We can share our very selves. I think perhaps sharing is a gift from the heart, while our next word, *giving*, is more a material gift.

Scripture Verses for Share

- I pray that you may be active in sharing your faith so that you will have a full understanding of every good thing we have in Christ. Your love has given me great encouragement, because you, brother, have refreshed the hearts of the saints. Philemon 6-7

- "His master replied, 'Well done, good and faithful servant! You have been faithful with a few things; I will put you in charge of many things. Come and share in your master's happiness! Matthew 25:21

- I have given them the glory that you gave me, that they may be one as we are one: I in them, and you in me. John 17:22-23a

GIVE

I believe giving in this context is handing something tangible to a friend, or person in need. It's filling a physical need. Jesus *gave* his all for us. There is no greater example.

When I was in high school, a poster on the social studies office window read: "*The smallest good deed is better than the grandest good intention.*"

Simply put, help someone, even in a small way, or maybe in an enormous way. Help others. God GAVE his Son. Christ GAVE his life. We are called to GIVE too.

Scripture Verses for Give

- Remember this: Whoever sows sparingly will also reap sparingly and whoever sows generously will also reap generously. Each man should give what he has decided in his heart to give, not reluctantly or under compulsion, for God loves a cheerful giver. 2 Corinthians 9:6-7

- Freely you have received, freely give. Matthew 10:8

- Give, and it will be given to you. Luke 6:38

- It is more blessed to give than to receive. Acts 20:35

REJOICE

Be thankful. Rejoice in what God has given you in every circumstance. It's his command.

I collect stories of how God helps us. [vii] Story after story, I hear tragic tales ending with the person telling me how much mercy they felt and how thankful they are for God's hand to have been on them. I shouldn't find this amazing, but I do. They don't want to re-live the circumstance or event but would never want to miss the closeness to God they gained through it. For them, this realization comes back as praise to God, rejoicing in his love.

These past few months, I've been forced to be still due to a knee surgery that developed complications. It's a small thing compared to what millions of people are facing today, yet, I'm incredibly frustrated (and more than aggravated) when I must climb stairs carefully and more slowly than I' like.

But I am also thankful that God has stopped me in my tracks, so I am required to sit still. *In the stillness, I find focus.* So, with a swollen knee, I open my computer to share with you what he has shared with me. I'm humbled and prayerful that it may give you hope and courage, and perhaps a new way to think about his love. I don't do *still* very well, but I'm blessed that he is making me sit and think about how he wants me to live my life. I *rejoice* in this unplanned restraining time.

Scripture Verses for Rejoice

- Everyone who is called by my name, whom I created for my glory, whom I formed and made...the people I formed for myself that they may proclaim my praise. Isaiah 43:7 & 21

- Rejoice in the Lord always. I will say it again: Rejoice! Philippians 4:4

- Rejoice always, pray continually, give thanks in all circumstances; for this is God's will for you in Christ Jesus. 1 Thessalonians 5:16-18

PLAY

One would think this would be self-explanatory, and it is for our boys—as they live entirely in the "play now, work later" mantra. But I was raised by German/English self-employed parents who ingrained in their children that you play after ALL the work is finished. Problem is, *the work is never finished.* So, God is kind to me in adding the word 'Play' to my list. As a result, I need to listen to God and accept his permission - to play and do something I love, explore someplace new, do something I didn't know I could do yesterday. Oh gosh—have fun and play because our physical life won't be forever.

"Your life is written in risks, the ones you took, the ones you didn't. Twenty years from now, you'll be more disappointed about the risks you didn't take than the ones you did." [viii]

This quote is not mine, I wrote it in my journal, but I didn't note the source. However, it is so true that I still feel its power. *The risks we take in life are what make it fun!* They are the adventure, the playtime. The chances are what keep our blood flowing and add depth to our lives. Take the risk, learn to kayak, hike the Appalachian Trail, and learn to do yoga or blow on a shofar horn, commit to teach vegetarian cooking or take a class. Do something *today* that makes your heart happy. Your Abba father encourages you. Your work will always be there when you're done playing. I think maybe the millennials have it right. They seem to understand the value of "play".

Even as I write this, I'm irritated at my 10-month-old, 70-pound puppy, because it's 8:10 pm and he wants to play, and I want to write. Then I look at him and laugh: a big lug of a pup, and I'm glad God gave him to our family. He is a gift of laughter and release; this dumb dog makes me pause and play. He's fun.

But if I enjoy having fun so much, why don't I let myself play more often? When I really dig deep, I'm ashamed to admit - *I*

like the feeling of being accomplished more than being refreshed.
But God doesn't want us worn and ragged; He wanted his kids
happy and revived in him. So, I must ask myself, "Is Jesus my
Lord?" or "Is he just on my To-Do List?" I'm ashamed at how
I honestly answer this. I've even convinced myself it is okay to
cross "Pray" off this ridiculous to-do list. I realize I have a
problem, but I don't think I'm alone.

God is filling our lives with delightful things to refresh us, if
only we would pause and enjoy them. Every elementary school
teacher knows the value of giving kids a recess—a time to play
and be recharged. The same is true for us. Ring the bell, take
the break, run and play so you can be refreshed. Our time is
not guaranteed, and our world is in upheaval. So, in-between
the chaotic events, when we have the chance - we need to relish
the moment and go play.

Scripture Verses for Play

- David and all the Israelites were celebrating with all their
  might before God, with songs and with harps, lyres,
  tambourines, cymbals, and trumpets. 1 Chronicles 13:8

- And David and all Israel played before God with all their
  might, and with singing and with harps, and with

psalteries, and with timbrels, and with cymbals, and with trumpets. 1 Chronicles 13:8 (KJV)

- That each of them may eat and drink and find satisfaction in all their toil – this is the gift of God. Ecclesiastes 3:13

- You are slaves to the one whom you obey. Romans 6:16

ENJOY ME - ENJOY LIFE

In A.W. Tozer's timeless book, *The Knowledge of the Holy*, he captures this gift of enjoying God and enjoying life. He writes:

God's gifts in nature have their limitations. They are finite because they have been created, but the gift of eternal life in Christ Jesus is as limitless as God. The Christian man possesses God's own life and shares His infinitude with Him. In God, there is life enough for all and time enough to enjoy it. [ix]

Our life *is our time*. And our father loves to look at his kids living in joy and peace, and simply enjoying one another in the time he gives us. Most earthly parents have this wish in their hearts too that their kids get along and enjoy life together. He provides us with the structure of time, so we have some mode in which to enjoy him and a framework of sorts, in which to enjoy life. In Heaven, there is no time, but we need it here on earth, so we have something in which to function. Years ago, I made up this little acronym for TIME...**T**ill **I** **M**eet **E**ternity. I believe time is a spacer, so to speak until we meet eternity. So, enjoy yourself in the time allotted.

Enjoy ME

God wants us to enjoy him and spend time with him. The Bible is full of funny stories and incredible teachings. One funny example I love is from the story of Moses with the Ten Commandments. Can you imagine, poor Moses smashed the first Ten Commandments and had to go back up the mountain to get the second set. [x] Just picture God talking to him in this "teachable moment". Perhaps it went something like this: "Okay son, let's try this again. But this time, we'll put them in a box, so you can't smash them!" Hence, the Ark of the Covenant came into existence.

God has such a sense of humor! He makes me laugh as I see myself in the story of Noah and the Ark. Just as God has all the animals and everyone on board, he waits 7 days to close the door. [xi] I like to think it's because he knew Mrs. Noah would need to run back and forth a few times to get all the things she forgot! What mom hasn't done that a million times? Some things never change. Almost daily, I run back into the house from the car to get something I forgot!

Another way to enjoy God is to simply enjoy one another! You see, God created this beautiful earth for us to live on, and he created the people for us to know and share life with. He gave us his Word that we may get to know him, and he created all of creation and beyond for our wellbeing and enjoyment. He wants the best for us. He desires for us to enjoy the life he gives; each day is a blessed gift.

Enjoy Life

I often must tell myself to savor; don't gulp life. I need to just enjoy this moment—it's all we have. But my internal mindset is always telling me to "Hurry up" and "Get it over with" so I can attack the next thing on my list. This must make God sad as I miss a lot of his great gifts as I rush past them. My life is incredibly blessed; I wonder how I can want to hurry, so?

When I was in 7th grade, my parents took my sisters and me on a wonderful cross-country vacation. It was the very first vacation I'd ever been on, and I was giddy. My sister and I sat in the back seat; she had the window, but honestly, she missed the whole trip as she was reading *War and Peace*. My dad was so upset with her. He wanted to show her new and exciting things, but sadly, she ignored his gift. She was in the car, but she missed the trip.

Don't miss the trip. Be driven by eternity but enjoy the moments at hand. It's a present and a gift from God.

Scripture Verses for ENJOY

- Clap your hands, all you nations; shout to God with cries of joy. How awesome is the LORD Most High, the great King over all the earth! Psalm 47:1

- To the man who pleases him, God gives wisdom, knowledge, and happiness. Ecclesiastes 2:26

- So I commend the enjoyment of life because nothing is better for a man under the sun than to eat and drink and be glad. Ecclesiastes 8:15

- How great is the love the Father has lavished on us, that we should be called children of God! And that is what we are! 1 John 3:9

SING!

Singing can change the way we feel; it transforms the atmosphere in a room. It can calm you down or make you want to jump up and dance. Music can delight us, and throughout the Bible, God tells us to sing. Singing can make you happy, and it makes God happy when his kids are happy too.

According to the Book of Job, God's work of creation was done to musical accompaniment. [xii]

"Where wast thou," God asks, "when I laid the foundations of the earth...when the morning stars sang together, and all the sons of God shouted for joy?" Job 38:6

How cool is it that God listened to music as he did his work! We should do the same as it lifts our spirits and lightens our load. Singing simply adds joy to your life.

According to Leonard Bernstein, the best translation of Genesis 1:3 is not "And God said." He believes a better translation is "And God sang."[xiii] The Almighty sang every atom into existence, and every atom echoes that original melody in three-part harmony by Father, Son, and the Holy Spirit.

May we glorify God the Father, Jesus Christ, and the Holy Spirit in our songs.

Scripture Verses for SING!

- Sing to him, sing praise to him; tell of his wonderful acts. 1 Chronicles 16:9

- Sing joyfully to the Lord, you righteous; it is fitting for the upright to praise him. Psalm 33:1

- Sing praises to God, sing praises; sing praises to our King, sing praises. Psalm 47:6

- "The LORD your God is with you, he is mighty to save. He will take great delight in you, he will quiet you with his love, he will rejoice over you with singing." Zephaniah 3:17

Thank you for allowing me to share my heart with you so openly. I feel blessed that God gave me these nine words as a roadmap on how to live well and bring him pleasure. I am hopeful they give you a bit of direction too. I pray that you remember the nine words, share them with your family and friends, and delight in how much God loves you.

Remember:

1. Focus on HIM - **Pray, Love, & Believe**

2. Focus on OTHERS - **Share, Give, & Rejoice**

3. Focus on LIFE - **Play, Enjoy ME - Enjoy Life, & SING!**

I pray that you may find your joy in him and delight in the life he's given you.

May you share his blessing well.

3rd Message

A New Way to Think About the Armor of God

The Armor of God as written in Scripture

¹⁰ Finally, be strong in the Lord and in his mighty power. ¹¹ Put on the full armor of God, so that you can take your stand against the devil's schemes. ¹² For our struggle is not against flesh and blood, but against the rulers, against the authorities, against the powers of this dark world and against the spiritual forces of evil in the heavenly realms. ¹³ Therefore put on the full armor of God, so that when the day of evil comes, you may be able to stand your ground, and after you have done everything, to stand. ¹⁴ Stand firm then, with the **belt of truth** buckled around your waist, with the **breastplate of righteousness** in place, ¹⁵ and with your **feet fitted with the readiness** that comes from the gospel of peace. ¹⁶ In addition to all this, take up the **shield of faith**, with which you can extinguish all the flaming arrows of the evil one. ¹⁷ Take the **helmet of salvation** and the **sword of the Spirit**, which is the word of God.

¹⁸ And **pray in the Spirit** on all occasions with all kinds of prayers and requests.

Ephesians 6:10-18

A Memorable Way to Think About the Armor of God

I truly wanted to remember the pieces of the armor God gives to us in Ephesians, but for the life of me, I couldn't relate to breastplates and shields. So, one day as I was praying, God gave me a fun way to remember all the pieces – as if they were rock climbing equipment! I suddenly found a way to understand the tools he's given us for our safety and protection, and more importantly, why he gave them to us.

- The **Belt of Truth** can be thought of as a **climber's belt** or harness. This piece of equipment connects us to the mountain, it keeps us secure if we lose our footing. It also gives an anchor that will stop us from falling. It often provides much needed balance and steadies us when we are on loose soil. We can trust the belt completely.

The belt of Truth, or climber's belt, is our secure connection to God. He wants us tethered to himself.

- The **Breastplate of Righteousness** can be thought of as a **bulletproof vest**. It protects us by giving cover for our vital organs, just like a good jacket will keep us protected from the harsh elements in a storm, the breastplate/jacket will keep us safe by keeping the evil of the world off our defenseless bodies, minds, and spirits. Jesus's righteousness is our cover; he alone is our protection. We can draw him close, zip into his care, and let him protect us. His goodness alone is our protective covering.

- Our **feet fitted with readiness** can be thought of as our feet in well-loved **hiking boots**. But I believe the big lesson here is the preparation and training one must do so you are always ready to climb the mountains in your life. You need to develop the stamina, so you can stand firm when needed. It goes without saying - you stand firm in your boots when you've practiced in them; when they mold to your feet, and you truly are comfortable in them. It is the preparation and practice that gives you confidence and peace when you are facing a trial. I love this quote from Oswald Chambers, it is incredibly true: *Preparation is not suddenly accomplished.*[xiv] So, break in your boots, you'll want to be prepared when you need supernatural peace in your life.

- The **Shield of Faith** puts a guard over our lives much like an **umbrella** keep the storms of life from drenching us. Obviously, an umbrella keeps the rain off, but in a similar way, the shield of faith keeps the invaders out of our lives. The umbrella, or the shield of faith, gives us hope of arriving at our destination intact. If you can imagine an umbrella that is much like a protective dome, letting nothing harm you... that is this faithful umbrella.

- The **Helmet of Salvation** corresponds to a **climber's helmet**. We all know, a helmet gives protection to our heads and to the brain God gave us. But more than that, this helmet gives protection deep within your mind, it protects your thoughts and gives you laser-like focus on what matters to God. When you put it on, you will know God's love for you. It will help you live your life knowing you've been given the incredible gift of salvation. This helmet helps you avoid distraction in a world that wants you fragmented with a busy schedule, multi-tasking every moment of the day, never thinking about things that are eternal. Put on the helmet - and clear the distracting fog.

- The **Sword of the Spirit** can be thought of as our eternal GPS **map, and its light** showing us the way to travel through life. It directs both the hopelessly lost soul and guides the saint. It is available to everyone and will lead them to joy and peace. This incredible map and its light gives each individual specific direction - for each day they live. It is a powerful supernatural guiding tool we'd be wise to follow as we travel through life. We need this map and its guiding light for both the mountain top experiences and the deep valleys we will experience in our lives. This wonderful map is the Word of God. It is always correct and relevant; especially when disasters strike and change our planned route. This map and its light are available to us even when the power goes out, or our batteries run dry. It is never changing, never needs charging, and is always up to date. It shows us the way to live pleasing God. It will lead us to our eternal home with him.

- The key piece of equipment is **Prayer in the Spirit.** It holds all the pieces of the armor in place like a magnet. It is a bit like **climbing ropes and cables** that secure the climber to the mountain, connecting them to the summit. But it's also a bit like a transcontinental telephone cable that lets you communicate with your leader just by thinking about him! It's amazing when you speak from your heart, and you are heard. Prayer connects us to God our Father instantly. Live clipped onto his climbing ropes, connect to his cable, listen for his voice, and be sure to thank him for the safety equipment he's given us for this journey.

Below are my CliffsNotes on how the armor offers God's love and protection:

ARMOR	PURPOSE	WHAT IT DOES
Belt of Truth	Gives BALANCE	Connection – secures us to God
Climbing belt		Steadies a person
Breastplate of Righteousness	COVERS us	Jesus covers & protects us
Jacket		Jesus's righteousness over us
Shoes of Readiness	Gives PEACE	Confidence & peace
Boots & Preparation		Being prepared gives peace
Shield of Faith	GUARDS us	Keeps invaders out
Umbrella		Is a guard over you
Helmet of Salvation	Gives FOCUS	Protects mind and thoughts
Climbing Helmet		Helps us avoid distractions
Sword of the Spirit	Gives DIRECTION	Shows the way to live pleasing God
Supercharged Map/Light		Applied Word of God guides us
Prayer in the Spirit	CONNECTS us	My Connection to God
Climbing Ropes / Cables		Communication with God our Father

Thank you again for letting me share the three messages with you, I pray they have blessed you as much as they are a blessing to me.

Remember, the big message from this small book is three-fold:

How to live in Awe as *you contemplate the Trinity* through the vision of the windmill.

How to live pleasing God following nine simple words, and

How to live protected by God when you put on his armor.

May you be richly blessed as you go forward and share his love.

Question for Deeper Thought

I pray that the following questions help you think about three things:

First, do you live in awe of God?

Second, do you live pleasing God with your life?

And finally, do you live under God's protection?

_____

_____

_____

_____

_____

_____

_____

_____

_____

_____

_____

Questions for the 1ˢᵗ Message:
An Ancient Windmill – A Vision of the Trinity

1. What is the stable anchor in my life?

_____

_____

_____

_____

_____

_____

_____

_____

_____

_____

_____

_____

_____

_____

_____

_____

_____

_____

2. Do I ever meditate on the awe-inspiring Trinity? How do I comprehend this reality?

Questions for the 2nd Message: *9 Words — What should I do LORD?*

3. LORD, what should I do with my life?

_____

_____

_____

_____

_____

_____

_____

_____

_____

_____

_____

_____

_____

_____

_____

_____

_____

4. When I pray, am I asking God, "What can you do for me?" or, "What can I do for you?"

_____

_____

_____

_____

_____

_____

_____

_____

_____

_____

_____

_____

_____

_____

_____

_____

_____

_____

_____

_____

_____

5. Am I worshiping or demanding when I pray?

_____

_____

_____

_____

_____

_____

_____

_____

_____

_____

_____

_____

_____

_____

_____

_____

_____

_____

_____

_____

6. Do I love deeply? If not, why don't I feel love?

7. Do I honestly believe Jesus is my savior, or *do I just think
I believe?*

_____

_____

_____

_____

_____

_____

_____

_____

_____

_____

_____

_____

_____

_____

_____

_____

_____

_____

_____

_____

_____

8. What am I willing to die for? What will I stand up for -
   no matter what happens.

_____

_____

_____

_____

_____

_____

_____

_____

_____

_____

_____

_____

_____

_____

_____

_____

_____

_____

_____

_____

_____

_____

9. What have I shared from my heart in the past few weeks? Do I share often?

_____

_____

_____

_____

_____

_____

_____

_____

_____

_____

_____

_____

_____

_____

_____

_____

_____

_____

_____

_____

_____

_____

10. What have I given from my time, talent or treasure in the past few weeks?

_____

_____

_____

_____

_____

_____

_____

_____

_____

_____

_____

_____

_____

_____

_____

_____

_____

_____

11. Make a list of what you are thankful for, then rejoice in his goodness, and 'Thank God' for his gifts.

12. Do I make time to be alone with God, to just be still and find focus?

_____

_____

_____

_____

_____

_____

_____

_____

_____

_____

_____

_____

_____

_____

_____

_____

_____

_____

_____

13. Do I like the feeling of being accomplished more than being refreshed? If so, what do I need to change? Do I want to change?

_____

_____

_____

_____

_____

_____

_____

_____

_____

_____

_____

_____

_____

_____

_____

_____

_____

_____

14. What do I do for fun? When was the last time I did it?

15. TIME – Till I Meet Eternity. Think about this – our days are numbered this side of eternity.

16. Do I know a story in the Bible that helps me see God's sense of humor?

_____

_____

_____

_____

_____

_____

_____

_____

_____

_____

_____

_____

_____

_____

_____

_____

_____

17. Do I savor or gulp life? Am I missing the 'trip' because I'm too preoccupied?

18. Do I have a favorite worship song? If so, sing it with all your heart, then rejoice in the joy it brings your Father.

_____

_____

_____

_____

_____

_____

_____

_____

_____

_____

_____

_____

_____

_____

_____

_____

_____

_____

Questions for the 3rd Message:
A New Way to Think About the Armor of God

19. How do I connect with God? Is he the steady balance in my faith life?

_____

_____

_____

_____

_____

_____

_____

_____

_____

_____

_____

_____

_____

_____

_____

_____

_____

_____

20. Do I truly believe Jesus has me covered? Do I rely on him for my protection?

_____

_____

_____

_____

_____

_____

_____

_____

_____

_____

_____

_____

_____

_____

_____

_____

_____

_____

_____

_____

_____

21. Am I prepared to stand up for Jesus? Do I have confidence and peace in my life?

_____

_____

_____

_____

_____

_____

_____

_____

_____

_____

_____

_____

_____

_____

_____

_____

_____

_____

_____

_____

_____

22. What is guarding my life? Do I have faith in God's promises?

_____

_____

_____

_____

_____

_____

_____

_____

_____

_____

_____

_____

_____

_____

_____

_____

_____

_____

_____

23. Do I protect my mind and thought life? What am I focusing on?

_____

_____

_____

_____

_____

_____

_____

_____

_____

_____

_____

_____

_____

_____

_____

_____

_____

_____

_____

_____

24. Do I read God's Word to bring clarity and direction to my life?

_____

_____

_____

_____

_____

_____

_____

_____

_____

_____

_____

_____

_____

_____

_____

_____

_____

_____

_____

_____

_____

_____

25. Am I connecting to God when I pray? Do I pray?

_____

_____

_____

_____

_____

_____

_____

_____

_____

_____

_____

_____

_____

_____

_____

_____

_____

_____

_____

_____

26. Do I invite God the Father, God the Son and God the Holy Spirit into my life?

In Unending Gratitude

First, I want to praise God himself, for literally pinning me down, and immobilizing my leg for the better part of six months so I'd take the time to do what I knew in my heart he wanted me to do. You see, on my own, writing just didn't fit into my to-do list each day, however I found plenty of time to take walks with my puppy, clean the dryer vent, sweep the garage and just about anything but write. I knew I was supposed to write and share what he had shown me, but I never got around to it. I'm ashamed to admit this, but it's distressingly true.

Please know that this has been a humbling task. I am not a Bible scholar, but I love Jesus, and he is faithful! I can attest to the fact that when he has plans for you, he will use whom he appoints, even if they don't feel qualified. I didn't feel qualified, yet he qualifies us all for our individual works. I can assure you that your skillset is not even considered when he gives you an assignment. Praise God; he fills in the gaps.

I pray this message will bless you and impact your life in a way that you'll want to share its messages and the Love of Christ with others. For you, this may be a new way to think about God's love. I hope it is, we all need something fresh from time to time.

I'm so grateful for my friends!

Even as God gave me these messages, he did not leave me alone to this work. I am grateful for many friends who encouraged me along this path. I'd also like to thank my handful of editors, friends, and family, who read, proofread, and offered suggestions.

I'm indebted to Edwina Patterson, lifelong author, and nationally known speaker, who encouraged me to keep my style when I didn't even know I had a style.

And my dear friend Lori Anderson, who even as she battles for her life, filled my spirit by her encouragement that what I wrote changed her thoughts of God and gives her peace in her battle.

I'm also in debt to Betsy Keith, who early on, encouraged me greatly when she said, 'She'd never think of a windmill the same again!'

And I'm blessed by my Church's prayer team as they kept me on their prayer list while they were on their knees before the throne of Grace, especially Julie and Dave Wilson, Phyllis Dangora, Phyllis Copponi, and Leslie Polcari, who kept checking on me as I was recovering. I just kept asking for prayer for my writing—I needed it. My leg needed prayer too, but I was more concerned that the writing would be worthy of you.

And my heart burst with gratitude for Rose Bonica, for her many phone calls, her tender heart as she shared with me what the writing meant to her, and for her skillful editing! An Italian immigrant at age 15, she has a self-taught command of the English language that would put most professors to shame.

And thank you, Kathy Dustman, for sharing your heart in what reading the manuscript meant to you at such a time like this. Your words of encouragement hit their mark.

I do want to thank my good friends in Massachusetts, Carolyn Durfey, Deb Fredette, Deb Flanagan and Mary O'Brian, who from conception to completion, have been my cheerleaders and prayer partners. And I am indebted to Charlotte Yates, Ann

Lamb and Ellen Grigsby for the final edit. Their attention and care are most appreciated!

I'm grateful for my sister, Rose Durham, who read my manuscript, gave good counsel, and allowed me to use her story in the nine words. Her perspective was completely different than mine, yet she was gracious on letting me tell it as I saw it from the back seat.

I'd like to thank Lori Anderson, Stan Keith, Edwina Patterson, David Wilson, and Lynelle Zandstra for such kind endorsements. Their words of encouragement gave my heart wings, and courage to take the next step towards publishing.

I am a bit at a loss for words as I try to wrap my head around the transforming work of Gracie Anderson who is an artist in the formatting world. Her work on the cover took the book to a new level and I'm in awe of her skill, professionalism and patience. You can contact Gracie on www.fiverr.com by looking up Gracie_Anderson. And I'd like to thank Kale Lange who is working with me on a children's book corresponding with *3 Messages from God*. He has been very instrumental in the final product and I owe him much gratitude for his insights and clarifying questions. He made our time working together a delight.

But most of all, I'd like to thank my husband, Carl. He knows too well how I go off on 'Wild and Crazy' paths every few years, yet he lovingly encourages me and listens to my wandering thoughts as I've pondered which way to present this message. I'd keep saying, "I'm not sure," and he'd listen and encourage, not once saying, "Sandy, who is your audience? What is your plan? How are you going to do this?" All of which I would answer, "I have no idea; I need to pray." He was my most steadfast encourager, and his love and care for me greatly bless me.

As you can see, even though I was alone recovering most of the time writing this little book, I was never alone. I am blessed to share life with some of the most exceptional people on the planet. I praise God for each of you!

With unending heart-ties to my friends,

Sandy.

PERSONAL NOTES

PERSONAL NOTES

PERSONAL NOTES

PERSONAL NOTES

PERSONAL NOTES

_____

_____

_____

_____

_____

_____

_____

_____

_____

_____

_____

_____

_____

_____

_____

_____

_____

_____

Works Cited & Resources

1. [i] A.W. Tozer. <u>The Knowledge of the Holy</u>. Page 35. Nashville, TN: Harper Collins, 1992

2. [ii] Edwina Patterson. 'Redeeming the Time Ministries.' PO Box 765, Lone Oak, TX 75453

3. [iii] Dr. James Denison. "Denison Forum" June 15, 2016. <<u>https://www.denisonforum.org</u>>

4. [iv] DAILY DEVOTIONAL. <u>The Word for You Today</u>. Knoxville, TN: Celebration Inc. January 3, 2016

5. [v] Oswald Chambers. <u>My Utmost For His Highest.</u> Sept. 10th, 11th &12th paraphrased. Nashville, TN: Thomas Nelson Publishers, 1992

6. [vi] Peter Marshall. 'If you don't stand for something, you'll fall for anything.'

7. [vii] Sandra Forsythe. Share God With Us, Inc. 2013 to present. <<u>https://www.ShareGodWithUs.com</u>>

8. [viii] Often attributed to Mark Twain but is disputed. 'Your life is written in risks, the ones you took, the ones you didn't. Twenty years from now, you'll be more disappointed about the risks you didn't take than the ones you did.'

9. [ix] A.W. Tozer. The Knowledge of the Holy. Page 72. Nashville, TN: Harper Collins, 1992

10. [x] New International Version. The Holy Bible. Exodus 32:19 & Exodus 34:1. Grand Rapids, MI. Zondervan Bible Publishers, 1996

11. [xi] New International Version. The Holy Bible. Genesis 7:7-16. Grand Rapids, MI. Zondervan Bible Publishers, 1996

12. [xii] A.W. Tozer. The Knowledge of the Holy. Page 157. Nashville, TN: Harper Collins, 1992

13. [xiii] DAILY DEVOTIONAL. The Word for You Today. Knoxville, TN: Celebration Inc. February 4, 2018

14. [xiv] Oswald Chambers. My Utmost For His Highest. Sept. 24th. Nashville, TN: Thomas Nelson Publishers, 1992

Made in the USA
San Bernardino, CA
11 March 2019